Gordon the Goat

retold by **Marjorie Newman**
Illustrated by Victor G Ambrus

OXFORD
UNIVERSITY PRESS

Gordon Goat was making hot soup.
There was a bang at the door.

Gordon Goat opened the door a little bit.
It was a big bad wolf.

"Go away!" said Gordon Goat.
"You are a big bad wolf and you want to eat me."

"I don't want to eat you," said the wolf.
"It's very cold out here.
  Can I put one leg in your house?"

"All right," said Gordon Goat.
"You can put one leg in."

"Can I put two legs in?" said the wolf.

"Yes," said Gordon Goat.

"You can put two legs in."

"Can I put three legs in?" said the wolf.

"Yes," said Gordon Goat.

"You can put three legs in."

"Can I put four legs in?" said the wolf.

"Yes," said Gordon Goat.

"You can put four legs in."

"Can I put my head in?" said the wolf.
"I was right," said Gordon Goat to himself.
"The wolf wants to eat me."

"Yes," said Gordon Goat.
"You can put your head in."
   He got his big sack.

The wolf jumped through the door and into the sack!

Gordon Goat tied up the sack and ran outside.

Gordon Goat climbed up onto the roof.

The wolf soon got out of the sack, but upset some of the hot soup.

"Ow!" said the wolf. "That's hot!"

The big bad wolf ran to get his friends.

"How can we get up onto the roof?" said one of
the wolves.

"I know,' said the big bad wolf.
"You get onto my back."

Gordon Goat was very frightened.
Then he had an idea. "I will trick the wolves,"
he said.

"Where is the hot soup to throw over the wolves?" he shouted.

"Oh no!" said the big bad wolf.
"Not the hot soup again!" He did not stop to think.

The big bad wolf ran away.
CRASH! The wolves all fell down.

All the wolves ran away and Gordon climbed
down from the roof. His trick had worked.

"Yum, yum!" said Gordon Goat.
"Lovely hot soup!"